Who Was Seabiscuit?

Who Was Seabiscuit?

By James Buckley Jr.
Illustrated by Gregory Copeland

Grosset & Dunlap
An Imprint of Penguin Random House

For all the underdogs in the world,
no matter what type of animal you are!—JB

To my brother Chris, for his influence, inspiration, and
support—GC

GROSSET & DUNLAP
Penguin Young Readers Group
An Imprint of Penguin Random House LLC

The publisher does not have any control over and does not assume any responsibility for author or third-party websites or their content.

Library of Congress Cataloging-in-Publication Data is available.

ISBN 978-0-448-48309-2   10 9 8 7 6 5 4 3 2

Contents

Who Was Seabiscuit?....................................1

A Runty Little Thing...................................5

A New Beginning.......................................16

The Perfect Team......................................28

Rise of the Biscuit...................................38

Big Wins and a Big Loss...............................51

The Fans Want a Race!.................................64

The Match Race..73

A Big Step Backward...................................81

A Triumphant Return...................................87

Seabiscuit's Legacy...................................94

Timelines..102

Bibliography...104

Who Was
Seabiscuit?

On a foggy morning in summer 1936, horse trainer Tom Smith stood by a Boston racetrack called Suffolk Downs. He was looking for horses that his stable owner could buy. Smith watched horse after horse walk by. The horses' riders, called *jockeys*, wore colorful silk shirts and bright white pants. The horses were nearly all tall, strong-looking, and elegant. They had long, straight faces and looked around proudly. Their breath came out in misty puffs in the morning air.

Smith had seen a thousand animals like them in his long career helping horses learn how to race.

As he watched, another horse emerged out of the fog. This horse was different. It was smaller than the others. Its legs were not long and lean. Its knees looked like they were different sizes. And instead of walking smoothly and proudly, the horse clumped along awkwardly.

But then the horse stopped. It turned to look at Smith. The trainer later said that the horse gazed down its nose at him and seemed to ask, "Who the devil are you?"

Smith just stared. In all his years of watching horses, he had never seen one like this. He had never had a horse look at him in just that way. The trainer, who had gotten his start tracking down wild mustangs on the western prairie, would always remember this moment. As the horse walked away, Smith said, "I'll see you again."

Two months later, Smith did see him again. Smith's boss, Charles Howard, had bought the horse. Over the next four years, Tom Smith helped the horse become one of the greatest racers ever and a real American hero. The horse's name was Seabiscuit.

Chapter 1
A Runty Little Thing

Seabiscuit was born in Kentucky on May 23, 1933. His mother was a mare named Swing On. His father was a famous horse named Hard Tack.

The foal (baby horse) got a name inspired by his father's. *Hardtack* was a type of bread eaten by sailors—it was a sort of sea biscuit. Seabiscuit had a half brother named Grog, born at nearly the same time, from another mother. Grog looked almost exactly like Seabiscuit.

Seabiscuit was a Thoroughbred. A *Thoroughbred* is a type of horse bred especially for racing. Thoroughbred owners try to match up strong horses. The hope is that they will mate and create more top racers. They match horses with great speed or success on the track to produce foals that can race and win.

Thoroughbred horses are usually tall and strong. They are bred from a long line of champions to be the best racehorses in the world.

But Seabiscuit was short and had lumpy knees. His head was not as long and sleek as most Thoroughbreds. He looked to some people like a regular pony, not the award-winning racing champion he was bred to be.

Hard Tack's father, Seabiscuit's grandfather, was Man o' War, one of the greatest Thoroughbreds of all time. Man o' War ran twenty-one races and won twenty of them. Horse experts call Man o' War one of the most perfect horses ever.

And his descendants carried on his success. More than sixty horses related to Man o' War won major races, and two were named Horse of the Year.

Hard Tack had a three-year racing career, and showed tremendous speed while winning big races. But he also had a terrible temper. He hated being put into the narrow starting gate. He bucked and jumped around before every race.

Finally, he simply refused to start one race, and his career was over. Gladys Phipps and Ogden Mills, the brother and sister who owned Hard Tack, and now Seabiscuit, hoped the horse's offspring would be winners—but not quite as grumpy.

With the blood of these great horses in his veins, Seabiscuit was supposed to be a winner, too. But when he was born, it did not look like he ever would be. Upon seeing the scrawny horse, one of the stable workers called Seabiscuit a "runty little thing."

Most young horses want to run in the fields, but Seabiscuit liked to do one thing: sleep. While nearly all horses sleep standing up, Seabiscuit spent hours sprawled in the hay of his stable.

But Seabiscuit was not bred to spend his days sleeping. Gladys and Ogden wanted him to learn to race. They asked James "Sunny Jim" Fitzsimmons, one of the greatest trainers in the country, to train him. If anyone could turn this sleepy colt into a champion, they thought, it would be Sunny Jim.

Sunny Jim Fitzsimmons taught Seabiscuit how to let a jockey ride him. The trainer put the horse onto the track for workouts and taught him to start a race from behind a gate.

But although Sunny Jim was a star, Seabiscuit was not. As a two-year-old in 1935, the grandson of Man o' War lost his first seventeen races. It began to look as if this particular Thoroughbred would not amount to very much at all.

"He was lazy," Sunny Jim said. "Dead lazy."

HORSE TRAINERS

LIKE OTHER TOP ATHLETES, RACEHORSES NEED COACHES. THE PEOPLE WHO COACH HORSES ARE CALLED *TRAINERS*. A HORSE TRAINER IS A COMBINATION OF COACH, PARENT, DOCTOR, AND FRIEND.

THEY ARE EXPERTS IN HOW HORSES RUN, MOVE, EAT, AND THINK. TRAINERS BECOME VERY CLOSE TO THE HORSES THEY CARE FOR. THEY ARE IN CHARGE OF HOW MUCH THEY SLEEP, WHAT THEY EAT, WHEN THEY WORK OUT, AND WHICH JOCKEYS WILL RIDE THEM.

TRAINERS ARE ALSO EXPERTS IN HOW HORSES' BODIES WORK. HORSES LOOK STRONG AND POWERFUL, BUT THEY CAN BE VERY DELICATE. THEIR HUGE BODIES ARE SUPPORTED BY VERY THIN LEGS. HORSE TRAINERS CARE FOR THOSE LEGS AND WATCH FOR ANY SIGN OF INJURY.

TRAINERS USUALLY WORK WITH SEVERAL HORSES AT A TIME. THEY TRAVEL WITH THE HORSES TO RACES AND ALSO ADVISE STABLE OWNERS ON WHICH HORSES TO PURCHASE.

Chapter 2
A New Beginning

Sunny Jim Fitzsimmons did not give up on Seabiscuit. He used his forty years of training to find ways to make the young horse run faster. One way seemed to work. During training runs, Fitzsimmons told the jockey to hit Seabiscuit on the side with a small whip.

This is not unusual in horse racing. Like any animal, horses want to run from danger or pain. Thoroughbreds are trained to run faster if they are hit with the small leather stick.

The first time they tried the whip, Seabiscuit burst ahead. He ran a quarter of a mile in 22.6 seconds, which was an incredible time. Sunny Jim knew then that Seabiscuit could run fast. He just had to get the horse to show it during a race.

Sunny Jim and his son, assistant trainer James Fitzsimmons Jr., decided that the answer for laziness was work. Seabiscuit ran race after race around the eastern United States. Occasionally, he would *place*, or finish second, but he didn't win. Finally, on June 22, 1935, in his eighteenth race, he won at Narragansett Park in Rhode Island. Four days later, he broke the track record for speed!

RACETRACK TALK

HORSE RACING HAS A LANGUAGE ALL ITS OWN. HERE ARE SOME OF THE MOST IMPORTANT WORDS TO KNOW:

CLAIMING: A RACE AFTER WHICH ANY HORSE CAN BE BOUGHT FOR A PRICE THAT HAS BEEN AGREED ON BEFOREHAND

FAVORITE: THE HORSE THAT IS EXPECTED TO WIN

GROOM: AN ASSISTANT TO THE TRAINER WHO HELPS CARE FOR A HORSE

HANDICAP: A RACE THAT INCLUDES HORSES OF DIFFERENT LEVELS OF SPEED—FAST, SLOW, AND EVEN—TO MAKE THE RACE MORE EQUAL

JOCKEY: THE HORSE'S RIDER

PLACE: TO FINISH SECOND

PURSE: THE PRIZE MONEY AWARDED TO THE WINNING HORSE'S OWNER

SHOW: TO FINISH THIRD

STAKES: A RACE IN WHICH OWNERS HAVE TO PAY TO ENTER THEIR HORSES

WINNER'S CIRCLE: THE PLACE AT THE EDGE OF THE TRACK WHERE HORSE OWNERS RECEIVE THEIR WINNING TROPHIES

But Seabiscuit did not make a habit of winning.
Out of thirty-five races in 1935, two-year-old
Seabiscuit only won five times. Seabiscuit's owners
expected more success. Other horses owned by

Gladys and Ogden were competing at the top level and winning often. So they tried to sell Seabiscuit. They put him in claiming races that had very low sale prices. Although he could be fast, he was also hot-tempered. Seabiscuit was acting like his hard-to-handle father. No one wanted to buy him.

In August 1936, Charles and Marcela Howard watched Seabiscuit run to a rare victory at Saratoga Race Course in New York. The Howards, horse owners from California, liked the shaggy-looking winner. They called their trainer, Tom Smith, to take a look at Seabiscuit.

Tom walked into the horse's stall and instantly
remembered the animal that had stared him down
earlier in Boston. This was the horse he knew he
would "see again." He saw something in Seabiscuit
that others did not, and he was sure that he could
make the horse a winner. He told the Howards,

"Get me that horse. He has real stuff in him. I can improve him. I'm positive."

The Howards, too, were impressed. As they examined him, Seabiscuit playfully bumped Charles Howard with his head. "I fell in love with him right then and there," Howard said.

The Howards bought Seabiscuit for $8,000, a
very low price for a Thoroughbred, even in 1936.
They sent Seabiscuit and Tom Smith to live and
work at a racetrack on the Detroit Fairgrounds.

There, Tom started training Seabiscuit in a new way. Instead of the whip, he used kindness. Instead of working the animal hard in race after race, he let him sleep. He fed him carrots and whispered to him. He fed him a different kind of hay, called *timothy*, for extra strength and weight. He also covered the horse's legs with thick pads soaked in *liniment*, a type of medical oil.

To calm Seabiscuit, who could be grumpy and mean, Tom got him some friends. Often, horses just want company. At first, Seabiscuit did not like the idea. A goat named Whiskers was brought in, but Seabiscuit tossed Whiskers back out of the stall!

Next, Smith brought in a large yellow horse named Pumpkin. Pumpkin became a comforting friend. Soon a dog named Pocatell joined the team, along with a spider monkey named Jo Jo.

Seabiscuit had a new trainer, new owners, new friends, and a new future.

Chapter 3
The Perfect Team

Through late 1936, Seabiscuit flourished. Tom continued to give the horse everything he needed—friendship, good food, and gentle treatment. Seabiscuit still did not like to be in a starting gate, much like Hard Tack, his father, before him. Starting gates are very narrow, just barely wider than the horse.

The horses must wait in this cramped space for several moments before the start of a race. Smith took weeks to retrain Seabiscuit to be calm in the starting gate.

Tom was the perfect trainer for Seabiscuit. He had grown up riding mustangs in the desert and working with wild horses. He spent years moving from place to place throughout the western United States, learning about horses. He worked in carnivals, at racetracks, and on cattle ranches. He was a horseman through and through.

Tom seemed to be able to think like his animals, to really understand their feelings. In fact, he rarely talked to people.

Some who saw him around the stables thought that he was mute, that he actually *couldn't* speak. But for all the silence he gave humans, he spoke volumes to horses.

For their part, the Howards were the perfect owners. They let Smith do his job and work his magic. Charles Howard had made his fortune selling cars in California. His main ranch, called Ridgewood, was near San Francisco.

RIDGEWOOD RANCH

He and Marcela both loved horses and horse racing. And they had a special affection for their stumpy horse. The Howards could afford to provide Seabiscuit with whatever Tom said he needed. They began looking forward to racing Seabiscuit, but they needed the right jockey.

The relationship between a horse and a jockey is one of the most interesting in sports. Jockeys are tiny men, rarely weighing more than 110 pounds. They ride animals that weigh a thousand pounds, in tight packs, at more than forty miles per hour. One slip and they can fall and be crushed. It takes great courage, balance, and athletic skill to stay atop a speeding horse. But just staying on top is not enough. A great jockey becomes a teammate of his animal, not just a passenger. The horse and jockey learn

RED POLLARD

to trust each other, so that when a jockey gives instructions, the horse will listen. A great horse needs a great jockey. In the flame-haired rider Johnny "Red" Pollard, the Howards and Smith found the jockey they had been looking for.

Like Seabiscuit, Red Pollard had had a bumpy ride. He grew up in western Canada, wealthy and well-educated. His family had owned horses, so  Red had been riding since he was a young boy. But his parents lost all their money in the 1929 stock market crash.

Pollard was forced to take a job as a jockey when he was fifteen. For the next fifteen years, he bounced around from racetrack to racetrack. He was small, tough, and smart, but he had never found just the right horse for him.

THE STOCK MARKET CRASH AND THE GREAT DEPRESSION

ON OCTOBER 29, 1929, THE NEW YORK STOCK MARKET CRASHED. THAT MEANT THAT BILLIONS OF DOLLARS IN INVESTED MONEY WERE LOST ALMOST OVERNIGHT. THIS LED TO MILLIONS OF PEOPLE LOSING THEIR LIFE'S SAVINGS, THEIR JOBS, AND THEIR HOMES. STORES AND FACTORIES WENT OUT OF BUSINESS. EVEN BANKS CLOSED, LEAVING FAMILIES PENNILESS. IT WAS THE WORST FINANCIAL DISASTER IN HISTORY.

AMERICA AND MUCH OF THE WORLD ENTERED THE GREAT DEPRESSION. THROUGHOUT MOST OF THE 1930S, MANY AMERICANS STRUGGLED TO MAKE ENDS MEET. MEN TOOK ANY WORK THEY COULD GET. SOUP KITCHENS FED MILLIONS OF PEOPLE. IT TOOK MANY AMERICANS MORE THAN A DECADE OF STRUGGLE TO RECOVER FROM THE FINANCIAL HARDSHIPS OF THE GREAT DEPRESSION.

In late August 1936, Red Pollard was in Detroit. He went from stable to stable asking for work. In the last stable he visited, he found Tom Smith and Seabiscuit. After speaking with Tom, Red walked over to the horse and held out a sugar cube.

Instead of turning away, Seabiscuit seemed pleased. He nibbled the cube and Red petted him gently.

Tom felt that there was something special about Red. It was the same way he had felt when he'd first met Seabiscuit. This was the jockey he was searching for. He hired Red Pollard on the spot.

Horse, trainer, and jockey began working closely

together. They trained in the mornings and relaxed in the afternoons, quickly becoming friends. Red learned the habits and riding style of Seabiscuit, whom he called "Pops." He began to see what Tom had seen in the animal. After one workout, he jumped off and told Tom, "This horse can win the Santa Anita," which was the race with the biggest purse in America.

With the right team finally in place, could an underdog racehorse become a winner?

Chapter 4
Rise of the Biscuit

The biggest race of 1936 in Detroit was the
Governor's Handicap in September. More than
twenty-eight thousand people packed Detroit
Race Track to watch. No one expected Seabiscuit

to do well. Popular horses, such as Professor Paul, were getting the most attention from people betting on the race.

Seabiscuit and Red were not bothered at all by the lack of interest. Trailing midway through the race, Pollard urged Seabiscuit to speed up. This was a big moment. In the past, the sometimes lazy horse was usually just happy to run with the pack.

But this time, with a jockey he trusted, Seabiscuit responded. He sped up and reached the leaders of the race. A few strides later, he was in front! Professor Paul tried to catch up, but he couldn't. Seabiscuit and Red crossed the finish line in first place. It was the fiftieth race of Seabiscuit's career, but it was his biggest win so far.

Tom Smith saw the energy he had seen in the horse's eyes way back in Boston. Seabiscuit was a champion who just needed to be guided the right way.

Charles Howard decided to take his new winner home to California. He hired a special railroad car and covered its floor with hay. For the next several days, the train chugged across the country as Seabiscuit slept soundly. When the train stopped occasionally, he came out to stretch his legs at fields near the tracks.

When they arrived in California, Seabiscuit
moved to a track called Tanforan near San
Francisco. After settling his horse into a new stable,
Tom brought Seabiscuit to the track for a workout.
He told the rider to let Seabiscuit go as fast as he
wanted. He was shocked to watch the horse race
a mile in one minute and thirty-six seconds. The
Tanforan track record up to this point had been

one minute and thirty-eight seconds. Seabiscuit had beaten the record just warming up! What could he do with a pack of horses to beat?

Everyone found out at the Bay Bridge Handicap race in November. Against a top field of horses, Seabiscuit did it again, officially setting the record at one minute and thirty-six seconds.

With Seabiscuit back in California, a trip to Santa Anita Park was the next move. The track there, located near Los Angeles, had been built in 1934. Betting on horse races had been illegal in

SANTA ANITA PARK

many states in the 1920s, and the sport had fallen in popularity. During the Great Depression, states looked for new ways to make money. They made betting on races legal again. California businessmen built Santa Anita to take advantage of the new law.

Though most people had little extra money, the chance of winning big attracted millions of bettors. The owners of winning racehorses took home the really big  prize money. But bettors who chose wisely could also make a lot of money. It was that dream that drove many to the track to bet.

To draw attention to the track, its owners

created the Santa Anita Handicap, a race that
awarded the winning horse's owner $100,000.
The race was nicknamed the "Hundred-Grander."
A *grand* is a nickname for a thousand dollars.
That "hundred grand" was the highest purse in
the world, worth more than $7 million in today's
money.

In the weeks leading up to the Hundred-
Grander, Seabiscuit beat another top horse
called Rosemont in a race. But in the very next
race, he lost badly to Rosemont. The two horses
were well-matched.

ROSEMONT

People wondered who would be ahead during their final rematch on February 27: the 1937 Santa Anita Handicap.

It was a clear day as the horses gathered for the Hundred-Grander. More than sixty thousand people packed the track. Radio announcers were ready to *call the race*—to describe it—for people listening at home.

A huge roar went up as the horses burst out of the starting gate. Red rode Seabiscuit through a

THE RISE OF RADIO

IN THE 1930S, RADIO WAS THE MOST POPULAR WAY FOR PEOPLE IN AMERICA TO GET NEWS AND ENTERTAINMENT. OVER THE COURSE OF THE DECADE, RADIO OWNERSHIP MORE THAN DOUBLED: NINE OUT OF TEN FAMILIES OWNED A RADIO.

RADIO WAS A SHARED EXPERIENCE. FAMILIES GATHERED TOGETHER NIGHTLY AROUND THEIR LARGE HOME RADIOS. A RADIO BROADCAST COULD UNITE MILLIONS OF PEOPLE, ALL LISTENING TO THE SAME THING AT THE SAME TIME.

RADIO SHOWS INCLUDED NEWS, DRAMAS, COMEDIES, AND LIVE EVENTS. HORSE RACING WAS ONE OF THE MOST POPULAR TYPES OF SPORTS PROGRAMS BROADCAST ON RADIO. THE RACES PACKED A LOT OF DRAMATIC ACTION INTO JUST A FEW MINUTES. AND FOR SOME, THE OUTCOME OF THE RACE WOULD MEAN MONEY WON . . . OR LOST. CHOOSING A FAVORITE HORSE TO ROOT FOR WAS A NATIONAL EVENT.

crowd of speeding horses. He found room on the outside of the pack and aimed for the lead. More than halfway through the one-and-a-quarter-mile race, Seabiscuit and Rosemont were out in front of all the other horses. It was a two-horse race. As the horses sped down the final stretch, Seabiscuit slowed down a bit. Rosemont caught up. Seabiscuit sped up again. Now the two horses raced at top speed. They blazed across the line, neck and neck. No one knew which horse had won!

Moments later, after studying instant photos of

the finish line, track officials declared the winner. It was Rosemont "by a nose." That meant that Rosemont's nose had actually crossed the line just before Seabiscuit's. After the race, reporters and fans blamed Red for slowing down Seabiscuit.

Red Pollard had a secret. Early in his career, he had been hit in the head in an accident on the racetrack. As a result, his right eye was blind. That blind eye could not see Rosemont advancing on Seabiscuit's right side, so he'd slowed down. If racing officials had known about Red's injury, he would not have been allowed to become a professional jockey. Red's secret remained hidden for the rest of his career.

Because people blamed Red for the loss, they continued to love and support Seabiscuit. That love and support would continue to grow in the months ahead.

Chapter 5
Big Wins and a Big Loss

Although Seabiscuit had lost the big race, he actually gained many new fans. People didn't blame the horse for the loss, they blamed the jockey. They began to read more and more about this little horse with the big heart and great speed. Like his many fans, Seabiscuit was trying his best to win. Americans saw something of their own struggles in those of the hardworking horse.

During the Great Depression, Americans wanted to be cheered up by the movies they saw and the radio shows they listened to. Popular entertainment thrived with happy rags-to-riches stories of regular people who became famous or rich or both. The story of Seabiscuit was no different.

At the movies, millions of people saw newsreels of the most popular horse races. On the radio, the races provided exciting drama for millions more.

New printing technology helped create weekly color photo magazines such as *Life* and *Collier's*. They all ran stories about Seabiscuit.

In the months that followed, Seabiscuit gave fans more to cheer about and reporters more to write about. After winning two more races in California, Seabiscuit took a train east to race on important tracks in New York, Maryland, and Massachusetts. He had little trouble winning there, too. By August he had won seven straight stakes races, one short of an all-time record.

Seabiscuit's winning streak thrilled the nation. Reporters flocked to the racetracks and stables to find out more about this star horse "from nowhere."

The fact that Tom Smith gave them so little news made them hungry for more. In fact, he held Seabiscuit's workouts in secret so reporters could not use stopwatches to report the horse's practice times. To fool them, he sent Grog, the Biscuit's brother whom Howard had also bought, out for workouts in public, which confused the reporters looking for "inside" information.

Seabiscuit's only stumble in a truly great year happened on a muddy track in Rhode Island. His winning streak came to an end when Seabiscuit came in third at Narragansett Park on September 11.

But that was just a minor stumble in a great year. Seabiscuit won more money and more big races than any other horse in 1937. However, a large part of the horse racing community still did not think he was the best.

For decades, Thoroughbred horse racing had been run by rich and powerful stable owners based on the East Coast. They did not think that Seabiscuit, from a California stable, could really be better than their East Coast champions. Their favorite was actually Seabiscuit's uncle. War Admiral was a son of Man o' War, Seabiscuit's grandsire.

In the summer of 1937, War Admiral had captured the coveted Triple Crown of racing, a series of races open only to three-year-olds. War Admiral was tall, sleek, and perfectly shaped. He was the picture of the perfect Thoroughbred. The East Coast racing owners could not imagine the less-than-perfect Seabiscuit beating their War Admiral.

WAR
ADMIRAL

Seabiscuit was now four and could not race
in any of the Triple Crown races. Fans, however,
wanted the two to race.
Newspapers demanded to
have the question settled on
the track. Radio announcers
longed to call the race.
But War Admiral's owner,
Samuel D. Riddle, refused. He felt it was
"beneath" War Admiral to race Seabiscuit.

THE TRIPLE CROWN

FOR MORE THAN A CENTURY, THREE FAMOUS HORSE RACES HAVE MADE UP WHAT IS KNOWN AS THE TRIPLE CROWN. THREE-YEAR-OLD THOROUGHBREDS TAKE PART IN THE KENTUCKY DERBY, THE PREAKNESS (IN MARYLAND), AND THE BELMONT STAKES (IN NEW YORK). A VICTORY IN ALL THREE IN ONE YEAR MEANS THE HORSE HAS WON THE TRIPLE CROWN. TO WIN ALL THREE, A HORSE NEEDS SPEED, STAMINA, AND A LITTLE LUCK.

THE FIRST TRIPLE CROWN WINNER WAS SIR BARTON IN 1919. SINCE THEN, ONLY ELEVEN OTHER HORSES HAVE CAPTURED ALL THREE RACES.

YEAR	HORSE
1919	SIR BARTON
1930	GALLANT FOX
1935	OMAHA
1937	WAR ADMIRAL
1941	WHIRLAWAY
1943	COUNT FLEET
1946	ASSAULT
1948	CITATION
1973	SECRETARIAT
1977	SEATTLE SLEW
1978	AFFIRMED
2015	AMERICAN PHAROAH

SEABISCUIT'S FIRST TRAINER, "SUNNY JIM" FITZSIMMONS, IS THE ONLY TRAINER TO HANDLE TWO TRIPLE CROWN CHAMPIONS.

Charles Howard and the public wore Riddle down. He eventually gave in and agreed to join a race with Seabiscuit. But bad weather forced Howard and Smith to keep their horse out of several such races. The teasing possibility of a big race made fans want it even more.

As the weather in the East turned to winter, Howard packed Seabiscuit back on a train to head to California. Instead of stretching his legs in empty fields, Seabiscuit arrived at crowded stops along the way. Fans gathered in the stations to get a glimpse of "their" champion. The people loved Seabiscuit.

He was a scrappy horse, struggling for what he could get, just like they were. It was a long trip, but a happy one.

As 1937 neared its end, sportswriters voted for the Horse of the Year. Seabiscuit had won more money than War Admiral and had won eleven of fifteen races. But the Triple Crown and the history of East Coast racing won out. In a close vote, War Admiral was named Horse of the Year.

In February 1938, Seabiscuit's team got more bad news. Red Pollard, like all jockeys, also rode other horses. At Santa Anita Park, Red was thrown from a horse named Fair Knightess. Red hit the track hard. Then the horse tumbled down on top of him. Red suffered many broken bones and serious internal injuries. He was nearly killed.

Seabiscuit would need a new jockey.

Chapter 6
The Fans Want a Race!

The Howards had to find a new jockey quickly. The big Santa Anita Handicap, the annual race Charles Howard most wanted to win, was coming up soon. Red suggested that his friend George Woolf ride Seabiscuit in his place.

Woolf was one of the greatest jockeys of all

time. He rode in fewer races than most jockeys but won more than almost any of them. He had an amazing ability to find just the right moment to make his move in a race. He was so calm and cool that his nickname was "the Iceman."

After he was hired by the Howards, George Woolf visited Red in the hospital. Red gave George advice on how to ride Seabiscuit. The two jockeys talked for hours, and George left knowing what he had to do to win.

GEORGE WOOLF (1910–1946)

BORN IN CANADA AND RAISED ON THE PRAIRIES OF MONTANA, WOOLF WAS ONE OF THE MOST TALENTED JOCKEYS OF ALL TIME.

WOOLF, NICKNAMED "THE ICEMAN," BECAME A PRO RIDER IN HIS TEENS. OVER THE NEXT FEW YEARS, HIS STAR ROSE QUICKLY. HIS FELLOW RIDERS MARVELED AT HOW HE SEEMED TO THINK WITH THE HORSE AND SEE WHAT WAS COMING UP NEXT IN EVERY RACE.

THE GEORGE WOOLF MEMORIAL JOCKEY AWARD IS GIVEN OUT ANNUALLY BY THE JOCKEYS' GUILD. IN 2010, A LIFE-SIZE BRONZE STATUE OF WOOLF RIDING SEABISCUIT WAS UNVEILED IN CARDSTON, ALBERTA, CANADA.

But when the race began on March 5, all the plans went out the window. Immediately after the start, Seabiscuit was bumped by a horse named Count Atlas. To avoid falling, George had to pull Seabiscuit back. As the horses gathered speed, Seabiscuit was near last place. Woolf urged Seabiscuit to get back up to speed. And in the next moments, Seabiscuit's legend grew.

From way back in the pack, he charged past horse after horse. "He's cutting the others down like a whirlwind," screamed radio announcer Clem McCarthy. For one stretch, Seabiscuit ran a half mile in 44.3 seconds. It was a world record . . . and it came in the middle of a race!

He was still behind, though. For the rest of the race, Seabiscuit ran neck and neck with Stagehand, another outstanding horse. The fans roared with every step the horses took. The finish line inched closer. Then, with a rush, both horses flashed past the finish.

The track officials studied photos and made their decision. Once again, Seabiscuit lost the Hundred-Grander by a nose. Most fans knew that had he not been bumped at the start, Seabiscuit would have been the clear winner.

"He tried with every ounce, every muscle in his body," Red said. "I am proud of my horse."

Once again, losing a big race did not make fans turn against Seabiscuit. In fact, he became even *more* popular! The well-loved horse's popularity during the summer of 1938 was later called "Seabiscuit-itis."

Over the course of the summer, Seabiscuit was on magazine covers and in movie newsreels. Fans could buy Seabiscuit board games,

"SEA-BISCUIT" BY BYRON

Seabiscuit Lady's Hats

pinball games, and even oranges named for their favorite horse. Ladies wore Seabiscuit hats. The

Howards dipped Seabiscuit's hoof in ink and "signed" autographs for him. Nearly forty million people listened to his races on the radio—more than a quarter of the entire population of the United States!

Seabiscuit

Red, meanwhile, was finally recovering from his injuries. He was out of the hospital and he visited Seabiscuit often. But in June, he took another horse out for a jog around the track as he tried get back into racing shape. The horse suddenly bolted at a loud noise and sprinted into the stables. Red was barely clinging on to the rampaging horse. As the horse rounded a corner, Red was flung off and smashed into a building.

His right leg was shattered. Doctors told him he would never ride again. Red, however, had other plans, and immediately set to work to try to prove the doctors wrong.

Meanwhile, the huge public interest in a race against the still-mighty War Admiral continued. On November 1, 1938, the day of the race arrived. George Woolf sat aboard Seabiscuit, ready to race against War Admiral.

Chapter 7
The Match Race

More than forty million people around
the country, including President Franklin D.
Roosevelt, were glued
to their radios. At
Pimlico Race Course in
Baltimore, the stands
were overflowing. Every
seat was full. The
infield, or center part,
of the track was opened
to hold the extra fans.

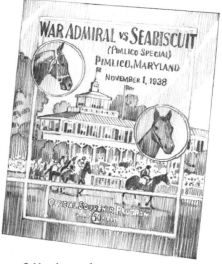

Trees around the track were filled with
people eager to watch the race. Even Seabiscuit's
old trainer, Sunny Jim Fitzsimmons, and his
former owner, Gladys Phipps, arrived to watch.

They were all excited about the race they had been waiting for: Seabiscuit versus War Admiral.

Most horse races include a large number of entries, sometimes as many as twenty horses.

This would be a *match race*, with just the two champions, one-on-one. War Admiral was well-known for not liking the starting gate. So his owner requested that the two horses be held by their jockeys behind a rope. He hoped this would give War Admiral an edge in the race, which would be 1 ³⁄₁₆ miles long.

But Tom Smith was one step ahead of this plan. He spent weeks training Seabiscuit to leap forward at the sound of a bell, the signal for the start of the race. For Seabiscuit, the gate or the rope wouldn't matter.

Red made sure that George Woolf was ready. He told his friend that if Seabiscuit ran ahead, he should let War Admiral catch up a bit. Red knew that if Seabiscuit got a look at his rival, he'd just run away from him. It was a bold strategy.

War Admiral's jockey was confident, too. "I don't think Seabiscuit will give [my horse] much trouble," said Charley Kurtsinger. "The Admiral will lick him."

Racing writers agreed with Charley. The *Daily Racing Form* was a very important horse racing publication. All of its writers predicted War Admiral would win. People betting on the race made the Triple Crown winner their favorite, too.

Seabiscuit's owner thought otherwise. The day before the race he said, "War Admiral [. . .] won't beat [Seabiscuit]."

Finally, the moment arrived. The bell rang, and the horses were off and running!

After a few strides, nearly everyone was amazed
to see Seabiscuit ahead. Smith's plan to train
Seabiscuit with the bell had worked.

The horses pounded around the track as fans on the infield ran across the grass to follow the action. The cheers from the massive crowd filled the air. As the horses rounded the first turn, Seabiscuit was in front. War Admiral was coming up fast on the outside. When they reached the next-to-last turn, the two horses were still very close. George did what Red had suggested. He let Seabiscuit slow just a tiny bit. The horse looked over and saw War Admiral. George called out, "So long, Charley!" then let his horse go . . . and Seabiscuit flew into a big lead.

War Admiral could not catch up. Seabiscuit galloped across the finish line well ahead of his rival. Waves of people poured onto the track, pushing past policemen trying to hold them back. They surrounded Seabiscuit and his rider.

A radio reporter managed to reach George Woolf. The jockey's first thoughts were for Seabiscuit's regular rider. "I wish my old pal Red had been on [Seabiscuit] instead of me," he said.

Charles Howard looked around the enormous crowd, which was still buzzing about what they had witnessed. He watched as reporters crowded around his winning jockey.

"He's the best horse in the world," Woolf told the writers. "He proved that today."

The writers finally agreed. Not long after the match race, Seabiscuit was named the 1938 Horse of the Year.

Chapter 8
A Big Step Backward

The joy of 1938 disappeared early in 1939. The Howards and Tom Smith were looking ahead to another race at Santa Anita that March. Seabiscuit was in prime shape and running well. On Valentine's Day, George Woolf rode Seabiscuit in the Los Angeles Handicap at the Santa Anita track. Midway through the race, the jockey felt Seabiscuit change his stride just a bit.

Woolf thought he had heard a noise from below him, too. A moment later, George felt the horse was in trouble. Seabiscuit was still running full-out, but his rider knew something was wrong. He tried to slow Seabiscuit down, pulling hard on the reins. Finally, Seabiscuit slowed and Woolf jumped off to calm the frightened horse.

Tom raced down to the stable to check on Seabiscuit. He and a track veterinarian looked at the horse's left *foreleg*—his front leg. The leg was not broken, nor could they see a bruise. But

horse's legs are very fragile. Tom wrapped Seabiscuit's legs and let his horse walk around carefully.

A few days later, the leg had not gotten better.

Another examination found the problem. Seabiscuit had hurt an important part of his lower leg. Horses with badly damaged legs usually cannot survive while the leg heals. In some cases, such an injury could be so bad that the horse would have to be *put down*, or killed. Seabiscuit, however, could still walk. But he could not race. All of his fans worried that their beloved horse would never race again.

Following the Los Angeles Handicap, they all returned to Ridgewood, the Howards' huge farm.

DELICATE LEGS

IN HUMANS AND OTHER ANIMALS, A BROKEN OR INJURED LIMB IS USUALLY NOT LIFE-THREATENING. BUT WHEN A HORSE SUFFERS A MAJOR LEG INJURY, THEY OFTEN CANNOT SURVIVE. ONE REASON IS THAT THEIR BONES ARE VERY LIGHT. WHEN THEY BREAK, THEY USUALLY BREAK INTO MANY, MANY PIECES. THOSE PIECES CAN BREAK THE SKIN AND CREATE AN INFECTION THAT CAN POISON THE HORSE'S BLOOD.

tendons & ligaments

bone

ANOTHER MAJOR REASON LEG INJURIES ARE BAD FOR HORSES IS THAT THEY NEED TO KEEP MOVING IN ORDER TO MAKE THEIR BODIES WORK RIGHT. THEY NEED TO WALK TO HELP THEM DIGEST AND TO TAKE PRESSURE OFF THEIR LUNGS. A HORSE CANNOT JUST LIE DOWN FOR MONTHS WHILE A LEG HEALS. AND THEY ARE SO HEAVY THAT CASTS OR SPLINTS WON'T HOLD THEM UP.

SADLY, MANY RACEHORSES THAT BREAK OR BADLY INJURE A LEG ARE PUT DOWN RIGHT ON THE TRACK TO SAVE THEM FROM SUFFERING.

Red Pollard was already there. He was living with Charles and Marcela Howard while his own injured leg healed. The jockey joked that he and Seabiscuit only had "four good legs between us"—three for the horse and one for the jockey.

The chances of a Thoroughbred recovering from such an injury were very slim. But the Howards, Tom, and Red were determined to try. For the next several months, both horse and jockey slowly got better. They began walking together, then taking short rides in the meadows and wooded

lanes of Ridgewood. Month by month, the idea of Seabiscuit racing again became more possible.

Charles Howard watched the horse in his stall one day. "You knew he wanted to race again, more than anything else in the world," Howard said to Red.

Finally, they felt that Seabiscuit was ready to race. In late 1939, they drove him to the Santa Anita track, with an eye toward trying once again for the Hundred-Grander.

Chapter 9
A Triumphant Return

Seabiscuit's first time back on the track was the La Jolla Handicap on February 9, 1940. His old jockey, Red Pollard, was on board. The tough rider had worked just as hard as his horse to get better. He made a special brace to help his healing right leg stay strong enough for the race. Doctors were not happy about his decision, but Red chose to ride.

In that first race back, Seabiscuit finished third. A week later, he came in fourth in another race. Fans were worried that their favorite horse was not as fast as before. Race experts thought it was Red who was not ready.

The final race before the Santa Anita Handicap was called the San Antonio Handicap. Tom felt that this time his horse was ready to win. He predicted that, "It's Seabiscuit, wire to wire," which meant being in front the whole race.

And Tom was right. Seabiscuit cruised to his first victory in more than a year. He was ready for the big race once again.

The 1940 Santa Anita Handicap would earn the winning owner $121,000—an enormous

amount of money. With the chance to see
Seabiscuit try for the prize again, more than
seventy-eight thousand people filled the stands.
Movie stars like Clark Gable, James Stewart, and
Bing Crosby were in the seats, too. And of course,
millions listened in on the radio.

Soon after the race began, Red rode Seabiscuit through a crowded field of horses. For a moment, he thought he would be penned in, unable to reach the lead. But a slim space opened up and he urged Seabiscuit forward. "Now, Pop!" he yelled.

Seabiscuit burst through. The enormous crowd filled the air with sound as "their" horse raced to the finish line. A horse named Kayak II, also owned by the Howards, caught up for a few seconds. But Seabiscuit stared at him . . . and then just ran away.

Seabiscuit flashed across the finish line, ahead

by a wide margin. No horse had ever come back
from a serious injury to win at this level. Red
Pollard's return to the saddle after his own injury
was just as remarkable.

Seabiscuit's team had finally done it: After
three tries, Seabiscuit was the winner of the
Hundred-Grander! Charles Howard leaped for joy;
Marcela Howard let out a shriek of delight. Even
George Woolf, who finished way behind Seabiscuit
on another horse, had to smile. When Tom Smith
finally reached Seabiscuit, he patted his horse.
Tom had known it all along.

With the win, Seabiscuit set a new record
among American horses for most money won in
a career: $437,730—nearly half a million dollars.
It was the thirty-third victory of his career in the
eighty-ninth race he had run.

As the crowed pressed in around them,
Scabiscuit was calm. He nibbled flowers off the
blanket of roses that was set around his neck. A
few minutes later, Red said, "I got a great ride.
The greatest ride I ever got from the greatest horse
that ever lived."

Chapter 10
Seabiscuit's Legacy

After the big win, the Howards retired Seabiscuit from racing. Seabiscuit was seven years old and had done all that was asked of him. He returned to Ridgewood, where he would begin breeding with *mares*—female horses—with the hope of fathering more Thoroughbreds.

The first foal sired by Seabiscuit was named First Biscuit.

In the next few years, more and more foals from
Seabiscuit were born on Ridgewood Ranch.
When they were old enough, they were trained
to race. At Christmastime, the Howards mailed
cards showing Seabiscuit posing with his "family,"
all the young horses he had fathered.

Unlike their father, however, most of Seabiscuit's offspring did not have much success. Sea Frolic, a *filly* (female horse), finished in the top three in eighteen of twenty-five races. A grandson named Sea Orbit won twenty-two races.

In total, Seabiscuit was the father of 108 colts and fillies. But none achieved the same success of their sire. Some horses racing today still trace their bloodlines back to the Biscuit.

As Seabiscuit enjoyed retirement, thousands of people came to see him. In his first few years at Ridgewood, as many as fifty thousand people drove over the ranch's dirt roads to visit him in the stables. They sat in bleachers near Seabiscuit's meadow. Sometimes, the horse would prance around, but most visitors remember him just sleeping in the shade.

On May 17, 1947, Seabiscuit died of a heart attack in his stall at Ridgewood. He was just six days shy of his fourteenth birthday, only about half as long as most Thoroughbreds live. He was buried in a secret location somewhere amid the trees on Ridgewood.

In 1949, *The Story of Seabiscuit*, a movie about his life, was released. It starred Shirley Temple, who was one of the most popular stars in the world. One of Seabiscuit's sons, Sea Sovereign, played his famous father in the movie.

SHIRLEY TEMPLE

SEABISCUIT, THE MOVIE

IN 2003, *SEABISCUIT*, THE MOVIE, WAS RELEASED. TOBEY MAGUIRE, THE ACTOR WHO BECAME FAMOUS FOR PLAYING SPIDER-MAN, PLAYED RED POLLARD. THE PRODUCERS USED TEN DIFFERENT HORSES TO PLAY SEABISCUIT IN THE RACING SCENES.

TO MAKE THE RACING ACTION AS AUTHENTIC AS POSSIBLE, TWO FAMOUS REAL-LIFE JOCKEYS HELPED OUT. GARY STEVENS PLAYED GEORGE WOOLF, RIDING AS WELL AS ACTING IN SEVERAL SCENES. IN THE BIG 1938 MATCH RACE, CHRIS MCCARRON PLAYED CHARLEY KURTSINGER.

SEABISCUIT WAS NAMED ONE OF THE TOP TEN FILMS OF THE YEAR BY THE NATIONAL BOARD OF REVIEW.

The Howards had a statue of Seabiscuit built at
the Santa Anita racetrack, where the horse had
had so much success. In the following decades,
though Seabiscuit remained well-known among
horse-racing historians, his story slowly faded
among the greater public. That changed in 2001

with the publication of *Seabiscuit: An American Legend*, by Laura Hillenbrand. The book was a best seller for months. In 2004, a movie based on the book was nominated for seven Academy Awards, including Best Picture.

Both the book and the movie brought the story of Seabiscuit back to life for millions of Americans.

As Charles Howard once said, "There will never be another Seabiscuit."

TIMELINE OF SEABISCUIT'S LIFE

1933 — Seabiscuit is born in Kentucky

1935 — Begins racing, loses first seventeen starts

1936 — Meets Tom Smith at a Boston racetrack in June
Bought by Charles and Marcela Howard in August

1937 — Loses Santa Anita Handicap in February, by a nose, to Rosemont
Wins seven straight stakes races in the summer
Wins more money than any other racehorse for the year

1938 — Lost Santa Anita Handicap in March, by a nose, to Stagehand
On November 1, defeats War Admiral in a match race at Pimlico Race Course in Baltimore
Named Horse of the Year

1939 — Injured in race at Santa Anita

1940 — In March, finally wins Santa Anita Handicap
Retires from racing

1947 — Dies six days before his fourteenth birthday, at Ridgewood Ranch in California, of a heart attack

TIMELINE OF THE WORLD

US stock market crashes, leading to Great Depression — **1929**

Huge dust storms begin to hit drought-stricken — **1931**
Midwestern United States. The "Dust Bowl" drives
thousands from their homes.

Amelia Earhart is the first woman — **1932**
to fly across the Atlantic alone

Franklin D. Roosevelt is elected president — **1933**
President Roosevelt starts a series of plans known
as the New Deal to help Americans recover
from the Great Depression

Civil war starts in Spain — **1936**

Famous mural by artist Pablo Picasso debuts; it depicts — **1937**
the Spanish Civil War and is called *Guernica*

Radio broadcast of fake Martian landing — **1938**
by actor Orson Welles starts a brief panic

Germany invades Poland — **1939**
World War II starts

Winston Churchill becomes prime minister — **1940**
of Great Britain

Japan bombs Pearl Harbor, Hawaii — **1941**
The United States enters World War II

D-Day landing in Europe by Allied forces — **1944**

Roosevelt dies; Harry S. Truman becomes president — **1945**
The United States drops atomic bombs on
Japan in August; Japan surrenders soon after

Jackie Robinson becomes the first African American — **1947**
baseball player in the American major leagues

BIBLIOGRAPHY

* Dubowski, Cathy E., and Mark Dubowski. **A Horse Named Seabiscuit**. New York: Grosset & Dunlap, 2003.

Hillenbrand, Laura. **Seabiscuit: An American Legend**. New York: Ballantine Books, 2001.

Nichols, William H. **Seabiscuit, The Rest of the Story**. Mustang, OK: Tate Publishing, 2007.

* Books for young readers

WEBSITES

ESPN Classic: "Size Doesn't Matter," by Mike Puma
http://espn.go.com/classic/biography/s/Seabiscuit.html

Seabiscuit: American Experience
http://www.pbs.org/wgbh/americanexperience/films/
seabiscuit/